We Watch Squirrels

We Watch Squirrels

Ada and Frank Graham
Illustrated by D. D. Tyler

DODD, MEAD & COMPANY   NEW YORK

For my husband, Hank,
and my friend, Debbie,
who mothered while I drew—D.D.T.

Text copyright © 1985 by Ada and Frank Graham
Illustrations copyright © 1985 by D. D. Tyler
All rights reserved. No part of this book may be reproduced in any form without permission
in writing from the publisher
Distributed in Canada by McClelland and Stewart Limited, Toronto
Manufactured in the United States of America
Designed by Jean Krulis

1 2 3 4 5 6 7 8 9 10

Library of Congress Cataloging in Publication Data
Graham, Ada.
    We watch squirrels.
    Includes index.
    Summary: Observes and explains the behavior of gray squirrels in the wild.
    1. Gray squirrel—Juvenile literature.   [1. Gray squirrel.   2. Squirrels]   I. Graham,
Frank, 1925-   II. Tyler, D. D., ill.   III. Title.
QL737.R68G69   1985   599.32′32   85-7075 | ISBN 0-396-08740-X

N

Contents

FOUR

Introduction

Watching Squirrels

You really don't need any special equipment for squirrel watching. Just a free moment, sharp eyes, and maybe a pocket filled with peanuts.

There have always been squirrel watchers. Some of them are scientists who share with us the things they see. Others are people who are curious about these little animals and enjoy learning more about them.

This book tells you what to look for. It tells you why squirrels behave the way they do.

Gray squirrels live almost everywhere—along streets, in the yards, and in the parks and woods close to where you live.

They are free for the watching. The things you read and see in this book can also happen right before your eyes.

Go out and see!

ONE

Nuts Tell a Story

Nuts in the park tell us a story. The round, thick-shelled hickory nut. The shiny, pointed acorn peeping from its little cup. The winged seeds of maple trees.

We know that we shall see, close by, the tall trees where these seeds and nuts grow.

Then, looking up, we are likely to see something else. Sitting on a branch, and staring down at us, is a small animal with a very long, bushy tail. It is the gray squirrel.

Now we have all the main parts of our story. We know that where we find nuts and trees, we find squirrels.

Summer is almost over. The days are growing chilly. We could say that squirrels carry an imaginary calendar that tells them fall is on the way. It is a busy time for them.

Squirrels eat growing things. Once in a while they eat insects and other small animals. But their favorite food is nuts, which are packed with energy.

Now, as summer ends, the trees have ripened all their seeds and nuts for the year. Each squirrel needs about fifty pounds of food to keep it alive and healthy through the late fall and winter. If each squirrel in the park buries that much food, well—there are a lot of nuts underground!

Squirrels are almost *everywhere* at this time of the year, finding and hiding all the nuts that have fallen from the trees. This is your chance to become a squirrel watcher.

Burying the Nut

A gray squirrel dropped from a branch onto the broad trunk of an oak tree. It hung there for a moment, head downward, its claws gripping the rough bark. Its wonderful tail, as long as the rest of its body, stretched behind it along the tree trunk.

The squirrel looked around to make sure there were no dogs or other enemies in sight. Then it walked headfirst down the trunk. It moved slowly through the grass, keeping its nose close to the ground and its tail high in the air.

The squirrel stopped suddenly. It had found an acorn. The animal sniffed the acorn, picked it up in its two front paws, and sat upright. It turned the acorn over and over and looked at it closely. What was going on?

Sometimes, when we open a nut, we find it is empty, or the meat inside has rotted. But the squirrel knew just by handling it whether the nut was any good. Perhaps the squirrel smelled the fresh meat inside. Or perhaps it could tell by how heavy the nut felt, or whether the meat rattled around inside the shell as it turned the nut.

The squirrel put the nut in its mouth, but did not try to eat it. It ran off across the grass, its tail now streaming out behind it.

When the squirrel came to a patch of bare earth, it

The squirrel put the nut in its mouth.

stopped and began to dig. It worked quickly, scooping up the earth, which grew into a little mound as the squirrel dug deeper.

When the hole was a little more than an inch deep, the squirrel bent over and pushed the acorn into the ground with its mouth. Finally, it used both paws to sweep the dirt back into the hole and pat it down. One acorn was safely hidden away.

Have you watched the little animal at work, putting food away for the winter? What special tools does the squirrel have, to find and hide its food?

The gray squirrel's front paws are different from the paws of most other familiar animals. A cat or a dog, a horse or a cow, seldom depends on its paws for eating. It stretches its head forward and picks up food in its mouth. Sometimes we see a cat reach out a paw to pull a bit of food toward it. But it doesn't bring the food up to its mouth with the paw.

The gray squirrel's favorite foods—nuts and seeds —are generally hidden inside tough shells. The animal must get at the food before it can eat. And it must be skillful at handling the food it is going to hide.

A squirrel uses its front paws much like we use our hands. Each paw has four long toes, like our four

Long, slender toes
are tipped with sharp claws.

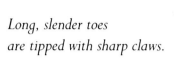

fingers. They are tipped with sharp claws. It even has a tiny fifth toe which looks something like a thumb.

These paws are strong, and armed with claws for digging. And these paws are nimble, so that when a squirrel picks up a nut it hardly ever drops it.

A squirrel buries dozens of nuts every day. It must be a marvelous animal, you say, to remember where they are all buried.

The truth is that a squirrel often forgets things, just as we do. After a few minutes have passed, it can't remember where it buried the last nut!

But the squirrel doesn't need a good memory. It depends on its nose, instead. All the squirrels in the park have buried nuts under nearly every tree.

When winter comes, and a squirrel grows hungry, you will see it scurrying across the ground. Its nose is down, its tail is high. It is searching for buried nuts.

Soon it will find one and dig it up. The nut may

have been buried long before by that squirrel, or by one of the other squirrels in the park. It doesn't matter. The squirrel will smell it and dig it up.

Whenever you see a squirrel in fall, it is likely to be hard at work—finding a nut and burying it, or digging one out of the ground to eat.

The Gray Squirrel

Now it's time to try to get a close look at this amazing little animal, the gray squirrel. We fill our pockets with peanuts and walk to the park.

The best times of day to watch squirrels are early in the morning and late in the afternoon. They are busiest then, at times when the sun is not too bright.

A squirrel is bounding across the grass, looking for nuts. If we hold out a peanut to it, the frisky little animal will see it. It will turn toward us and move in our direction.

The squirrel will stop, looking at us and at the peanut. When it has decided that we are friendly and will do it no harm, it will bound right up to our feet.

It stands on its hind legs, its front paws tucked in toward its chest.

Now we are face to face with a gray squirrel. We may get a good look at the squirrel, but the squirrel may not get such a good look at us. A scientist who has watched squirrels for years says that they pay close attention to our faces and the hand that holds the nut. But they may not even realize that our legs and feet are parts of us!

Up close we are able to see the short yellow hairs scattered across its gray face. The eyes, large and dark, are set on the sides of its head, where they do the squirrel the most good.

They are excellent eyes, able to see a long distance. Without even moving its head, the squirrel can search most of its surroundings, and even the sky above, for its enemies.

When the squirrel is alarmed, its eyes "bug out," pushing farther out from its head so that it can see across an especially wide area. But, because the eyes are set wide apart on the sides of the head, the squirrel has trouble seeing objects that are right in front of it. It may be standing close to a nut and not notice it.

The eyes help to protect the squirrel from its ene-

The squirrel stops, looking at us and the peanuts.

mies. But it depends on its nose for finding food.

Watch the squirrel's nose as it comes toward the peanut. It has large nostrils. You can see them move, fluttering and opening wide, as the animal sniffs for

When alarmed, a squirrel's
eyes "bug out."

It depends on its nose for
finding food.

A squirrel can turn its ears toward a sound it especially wants to hear.

food. That nose can smell nuts that are locked in a box or buried in the earth.

Notice the squirrel's ears. Often they are held straight up. But the squirrel can lay them flat against its head, or turn them toward a sound it especially wants to hear.

Even in fall, when a squirrel is busy burying nuts, it gets hungry and stops to eat some of them. A peanut doesn't have a tough shell. The squirrel will probably eat the peanut rather than bury it.

The squirrel's four front teeth—two above and two below—are special. They are incisors, as hard

and sharp as tiny chisels. They cut right through the toughest shells in a few seconds.

The gray squirrel bites hard on the peanut shell, quickly breaking it open. It peels off the thin brown skin, which comes flying out of the sides of its mouth in tiny bits. Then the squirrel's cheek teeth—or molars—grind the peanut into crumbs so that it can be swallowed.

In a moment the squirrel turns and bounds back toward the trees. It goes on with its busy work, finding seeds and nuts to fatten itself for the hard winter ahead, and burying other nuts.

TWO

Trailways

Winter has come to the park. The cold wind has blown away the leaves. We can see into the trees and discover what is going on among their branches.

The trees stretch away on all sides of us. They are like huge apartment houses. Squirrels dash up and down the trunks and branches, which are their stairs and hallways.

But when they want to cross from one of their tree houses to another, they don't have to go all the way "downstairs"—they simply leap from the top of one tree to its neighbor. We can watch this winter carnival of the squirrels.

A gray squirrel scurries out on a branch, giving us a good look at itself. Even so, it isn't easy to guess how long it is. Its bushy tail is almost as long as the rest of its body.

Let's guess that the tail is about eight inches long. How long is the *whole* squirrel? Eight times two, plus and inch or so? Most gray squirrels, then, are about seventeen inches from the nose to the tip of the tail.

Squirrels can simply leap from the top of one tree to its neighbor.

What else do we notice? The gray squirrel isn't really gray!

The little animal, stretched along the branch, matches the different colors of the bark. It wears a many-colored coat. Its chest and belly are white. The hairs on its head and back are yellow, brown, and black, all mixed together so that they look gray from a distance.

There are changes in the squirrel with the coming of winter. It has grown a longer, thicker coat of hair to protect it from the cold.

We wear earmuffs in winter to keep in the heat our body makes. It's a trick we have learned from animals such as squirrels. In winter, the gray squirrel grows tufts of white hair behind its bare ears to keep heat from escaping.

The squirrel flicks its tail and whirls around to face the trunk of the tree. In a moment it is gone, dashing along the travel lanes formed by the branches and vines over the park.

Part of the fun in squirrel watching is trying to guess what the animal is going to do next.

A squirrel runs along a thin branch, as easily as a tightrope walker in the circus. At the end of the

In winter, gray squirrels grow tufts of white hair behind their ears.

branch it stops. What will it decide to do?

The squirrel raises and lowers its head rapidly—up, down, up, down. It is trying to get a good look at the spot where it will land.

The branch bends under the weight of the squirrel. As the springy branch begins to snap up again, the squirrel leaps into the air. It is almost as if the animal had been flung out of a slingshot.

Feet outstretched, the squirrel flies through the air. The great bushy tail, stretched out behind, is like a parachute. The squirrel lands lightly on a branch twenty feet away.

The trees are full of squirrels. Each of them bounds

easily through the branches high above the ground. We have watched their nimble front legs and paws as they turned over nuts and buried them. Now we notice their hind legs.

The hind legs of squirrels are long and sturdy. We see the large feet grip the branches. We see the powerful muscles push the squirrel in exciting leaps from tree to tree.

The squirrels run along the branches, shifting their long tails from side to side to keep their balance. They dig their sharp claws into the trunks to keep from falling. If we look closely on the trunks of trees, we may see the long scratches left by those claws in the bark.

The squirrels seem to drift across the sky above us as easily as birds fly. They make us want to follow them.

But squirrels know the world of treetops. They have been running and leaping through those travel lanes in the air all their lives. They go where we could never follow them.

But we can follow them with our eyes.

Winter Storm

Squirrels hate cold, windy days. They vanish. If you go to the park on one of those days, you may not see a squirrel.

Naturally, you look for them. You may see scratch marks on a tree, about half an inch apart, showing where a squirrel's claws scraped the bark when its foot slipped. You may see old footprints still stamped in the frozen ground.

When you look up into the branches, no frisky, jumping, bushy-tailed creatures are in sight. Only, perhaps, an unhappy crow perched on a dead limb, its feathers ruffled in the wind.

Then, here and there among the branches, you see big balls of brown leaves. That's where the squirrels are hiding.

Those hiding places are called leaf nests. They were built by the squirrels months before, when the weather was still fine and the animals had no need for places to keep warm and dry.

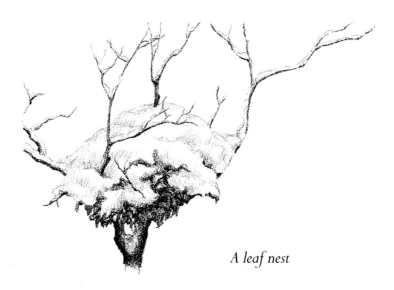

A leaf nest

Some squirrels stay warm in snug holes in the trees. But there are not enough hollow trees for all of them. So the other squirrels get busy in fall and build leaf nests for the cold, windy weather that is sure to come.

They choose a place on a strong branch or against the trunk of a tree. First, they build a floor with twigs and branches. Over the floor they put together a big ball of leaves and sticks about two feet across. They line the inside of the nest with grasses and strips of bark so that it is soft and warm.

On days when a fierce wind blows out of the north and ice coats the branches, the squirrels have no wish to go racing and leaping through the trees. They could not leap safely from tree to tree in high winds. They might slip and fall from icy branches.

As long as the storm rages, you will have a hard time finding squirrels. They are sleeping in their tree nests, with their great fluffy tails wrapped around them like woolen blankets.

The weather soon changes. The wind drops and the sun comes out. It is still cold, but when you come to the park you will notice the difference.

A call comes from the trees. It is a barking sound, but not like the bark of a dog. It is the bark of a squirrel sending a message to one of its neighbors.

All the squirrels are out today. The trees are full of sounds—the squirrels chattering and grunting and squeaking and purring.

A squirrel sits on a low branch, making an angry, rasping noise at somebody or something. Its teeth chatter and its little body heaves up and down. Above it, two other squirrels are carrying mouthfuls of leaves to mend a nest that was damaged by the wind.

Some of the squirrels have come down on the

ground beneath the trees. They need water every day and are thirsty after their long sleep in the nest during the storm.

But the water in the pond is frozen. One squirrel eats snow left over from the storm. Another reaches up to sip water from a melting icicle. Still another squirrel—one with a sweet tooth, no doubt—licks the sap that has started to drip from the trunk of a maple tree.

Patches of snow are crisscrossed by the tracks of hungry squirrels. A few lucky ones have found fat grubs, or the cocoons of insects, hidden in old logs. But most of them are bounding across the open spaces, their noses close to the ground, hunting for buried nuts.

This is a chance to see how good a squirrel is at finding hidden food. Watch closely! A squirrel stops in a patch of snow. It sniffs the snow, then begins digging furiously with its front paws.

The snow flies. Soon the frozen earth beneath it is scooped away, too. In a few minutes the excited squirrel pulls up a nut buried several months earlier.

That squirrel probably did not bury *that* nut. Once the nuts are in the ground, it is finders' keepers.

A squirrel licks sap dripping from the trunk of a maple tree.

The squirrel begins digging furiously in the snow.

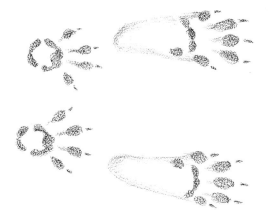

Tracks of hungry squirrels can be seen in the snow.

The buried nuts belong to the whole community of squirrels.

What happens to the buried nuts that squirrels never find? They sprout into trees! Many of the oaks and hickory trees in the park were planted by the squirrels themselves.

The Chase

Squirrel watchers hardly ever spend a boring day.

One morning, late in February, there is a new sense of excitement in the park. The trees seem to shake in a swirl of racing squirrels. If you didn't know what was going on, you might think all of the squirrels in the park had suddenly gone crazy.

A squirrel runs through the treetops, waving its tail to keep its balance as it springs from branch to branch. Four or five other squirrels chase the leader. They rush up the trunk of one tree and down the branches of another. Sometimes the leader leaves the trees and bounds away over the ground. The others come tumbling after it.

The great chase is on, and it has a purpose. The mating season has begun. The squirrel in the lead is a female. The males are chasing her, each one hoping that one day soon she will be his mate.

THREE

In the Nest

High above the park something exciting is going on. We cannot see it, because it is happening in the branches of a tall tree, inside a leaf nest.

Winter is coming to an end. The nights are still cold, and the birds have not yet started to build their nests, but buds are bursting open on all the trees. A squirrel is going in and out of the opening in the side of the leaf nest.

If we could look inside the nest, we would see four tiny creatures. Their eyes are closed and their bodies are hairless. They are squirrels that have just been born.

Late winter is a very busy time for the mother squirrel. If you have been watching closely, you have seen her leaping through branches in the tall tree.

Most of the nuts that were buried last fall are gone now. She and the other squirrels have eaten them during the winter. She comes out of the nest now to eat the fresh, juicy buds growing on the trees.

Watch for the squirrel hanging head downward from a branch. She is biting off fresh buds and flowers. You can see some of these buds and flowers lying on the ground under the trees. The squirrel runs down the tree trunk to eat them.

The mother squirrel must keep eating. She needs lots of energy to feed and take care of the four baby squirrels in the nest.

You may see her running through the branches, carrying a piece of bark in her mouth. She carries it into the nest. Still holding it in her mouth, she tears it into thin strips with her sharp claws. Then she mixes the strips of bark with leaves on the floor of the nest to make a soft bed for her babies.

The wind of late winter blows through the park at night. But the four baby squirrels lie close to their mother, snug under her bushy tail.

Inside the nest are four tiny creatures.

When only two or three days old, baby squirrels cannot see or hear.

Baby Squirrels

Daylight comes to the park. The baby squirrels begin to squirm in the nest. They make little squealing sounds.

The squirrels are still only two or three days old. They hardly look like squirrels at all.

They cannot see. They cannot hear. Their eyes are tightly closed and their ears are folded down like flaps on the sides of the head.

There is no fur on their bodies. They are completely naked, and their pink skin is so thin and clear that you can almost look through and see their tiny bones inside.

The baby squirrels simply look like small lumps in the dark nest. They are about three inches long, including the tail. They weigh about an ounce. But their mother knows they are there because she can hear them squeal when she moves.

The baby squirrels cling to her. Like all mammals, they take nourishment to grow from their mother. The nourishment is in the form of milk from her body.

The mother will be nursing her babies for a long time. They grow slowly. By the second week of their lives, they are about twice as large as when they were born. Thin fuzz begins to sprout on their backs.

The next week the flaps on the sides of the head begin to open and the baby squirrels can hear each other. They squirm more in the nest. When one of them pushes a brother or sister, that little squirrel squeals loudly.

When they are a month old, their little bodies are covered with fuzzy hair. The claws on their toes are growing sharp.

But the babies still can't lift their long tails. They push themselves to their feet, trembling all over. Then they wobble and fall down.

*When a month old,
the claws on their
toes are growing sharp.*

Another week goes by. The mother is busy nursing her babies and licking their new fur. She keeps the nest clean.

The squirrels' eyes are now open and they can see each other. They are beginning to look like squirrels! Their long front teeth—those teeth that will be so important to them—are beginning to grow. They start nibbling on bark and twigs and the other objects around them. Sometimes they nibble on each other's ears.

The babies are really little squirrels by the time they are two months old. They can hold up their long, furry tails. Their ears stand straight up like their mother's. Their eyes are wide open, big and shiny.

They move around a lot now in the nest. They push each other over, struggling and squealing to get close to their mother so that she can nurse them.

A young squirrel picks up a strip of bark in its mouth and begins to chew on it. Its long front teeth will keep growing for the rest of its life and it must chew often to keep them from growing *too* long.

At two months, the babies are really little squirrels.

The little squirrel wobbles and falls down. But it doesn't stop nibbling on the strip of bark.

Being a Mother

One day the mother squirrel was sitting on a branch near the leaf nest, eating a fat bud. She looked down and saw something that frightened her.

A long black snake came crawling up the trunk of the tree. It stopped on a branch just below the nest. The snake curled itself up and remained very still. Only its tongue moved, flicking in and out of its mouth.

Snakes often rob nests. They swallow birds' eggs and young squirrels. The mother squirrel sensed that her babies were in danger.

She dashed into the nest, making a little warning grunt. She already knew how she was going to protect her babies.

Quickly, the mother pushed one of the young squirrels over on its back. She picked it up in her mouth by the soft, furry skin on its belly. The young squirrel threw its four legs around her neck, tucking its tail over her back.

The mother swiftly left the nest. She held the young squirrel under her chin, pressed tightly against her chest. Then she started her trip through the branches of the big tree.

Where was she going? If you are very lucky, you may see the whole story yourself some day as a mother squirrel moves her babies from one place to another.

Squirrels are usually well prepared for trouble when raising a family. They often build two nests. They raise their family in one nest, and keep the other one ready for a time when they may need it.

Sometimes they leave the first nest if they sense that another animal will harm their babies. Or they may change nests if fleas or other pesky creatures get in.

Now the mother squirrel swiftly carried her baby to safety. She jumped from one branch to another and reached a nearby tree. There a new nest was ready.

The mother put the baby safely inside. Then she returned to the old nest for another baby. She made four trips, each time carrying a young squirrel care-

A black snake came crawling up the trunk of the tree.

fully under her chin. In less than half an hour, her family was out of danger.

The young squirrels went on growing in the new nest. They could not live without their mother's help. They came to her for milk when they were hungry.

As the days grew warmer, the squirrels began to come out of the nest. Maybe you will see the small squirrels, following their mother on nice days in late May.

All the squirrels eat hungrily. Even the mother squirrel begins to get fat after the hard days of winter and raising a family. One squirrel watcher saw a squirrel eat nearly a hundred elm buds as large as peas in fifteen minutes.

What do the squirrels in your park eat in spring?

Their mother always watches the young squirrels carefully when they come down on the ground. If someone in the park tries to pick one of them up, the frightened squirrel may set up a loud cry. The mother will hear the young one and rush to defend it. Her teeth are long and her claws are sharp. She may bite and scratch if she thinks the little squirrel is in trouble.

She is a good teacher. She has learned to avoid danger in the park. Watch what she does. When she wants to cross the road, she waits until no cars are in sight.

The young follow her, learning where to find food and how to avoid danger. Someday they will be frisky, adventurous squirrels, leaping from branch to branch high in the trees.

But it will take time. At first, they are afraid to follow their mother far out on slender branches or telephone wires. But she turns and runs ahead, coaxing them on. Soon they follow her everywhere.

They are learning to be squirrels.

FOUR

Learning to Be Squirrels

When you walk into the park on a fine summer day, you are in for a treat!

At first you may think the squirrels have a recess, and you are in the middle of a giant squirrel playground.

The young squirrels are very active now. They leap through the trees and hang head down from branches. They bound over the grass, poking lively noses into everything. They wrestle with each other, then suddenly turn and dash away.

But, as frisky as they are, the young squirrels are not simply playing. The long weeks in the nest are be-

hind them, and now they must learn to become suc-
cessful squirrels.

Young squirrels must get used to the sights and
smells around them. They must get acquainted with
those travel lanes above them—the best way to run
through the branches from the top of one tree to
another. One slip of the foot and they might be in
trouble.

A young squirrel sneaks up on her brother. She
looks almost fierce, as if she is going to leap on him
and capture him. But watch carefully. Suddenly, she
leaps the other way— just as if some huge creature
has tried to capture *her*.

Is this a game? Partly, perhaps. But that young
squirrel is getting practice in escaping from an enemy.
Someday, if a cat attacks her, she may have to move
fast.

Have you seen a squirrel up close? Did you notice
the shiny black whiskers on its face?

A squirrel grows whiskers not just to look pretty.
It uses its whiskers the way a cat does. Whiskers are
like radar—they send a warning in advance.

A squirrel may see a hole it wants to explore.

Young squirrels get used to sights and smells around them.

A squirrel uses its whiskers the way a cat does.

When it pokes its head into the hole, the whiskers tell the squirrel how much room it has.

Those whiskers are as wide as the squirrel's body. If they touch the walls of the hole, they tell the squirrel that it doesn't have much room. It had better be careful.

A young squirrel is always nibbling on something. A pinecone. A strip of bark. A small rubber ball. That's because a young squirrel is always learning. It learns what to eat and what it can't eat. It learns how to open a hard nut. It also learns not to waste time opening a rubber ball.

A squirrel keeps chewing, all through its life.

Squirrel Talk

Squirrels talk to each other with their hair.

When we want to let a friend know how we feel, we generally use words. We talk to them.

Squirrels make many sounds. They don't use words like we do, but they bark, squeal, chatter, purr, and grunt.

When a mother squirrel wants to warn her babies of danger, she makes a sharp sound like a cough. Then the babies lie still so their enemies can't see them.

Both people and squirrels also talk by signs. When we make a fist and shake it at someone, it means "Watch out!"

Squirrel watchers know that squirrels use signals, too. These furry animals use their hair to talk about things that are important to them.

When a squirrel is angry, it raises the hair on its back. The light tips of those hairs seem to flash like a light. They say to another squirrel, "Watch out!"

A young squirrel learns these signals quickly. Getting to know signals is a way to fit into the squirrel community.

Watch for these signals. They will tell you who is boss among the squirrels.

Drop a few peanuts on the ground. A squirrel will hurry over and start eating them. Then another squirrel scrambles down from a tree and comes to the peanuts.

The newcomer makes a signal. It raises its hair on its back. The first squirrel runs away. The newcomer has the peanuts all to itself. That squirrel is boss.

Squirrels have a "pecking order" in their community. One squirrel is always stronger than any other. It "pecks" other squirrels, or drives them away. It is number one in the squirrel community.

An old male is usually number one. All the other squirrels know who is strongest and who is weakest.

Female squirrels come next. There is a female stronger than all the others. The pecking order goes right down to the weakest one.

Young squirrels, just out of the nest, are at the bottom of the pecking order. They learn quickly where they stand. All the older squirrels, both males and females, can boss them around.

The pecking order is important to squirrels. Without it, they would waste a lot of time fighting.

An old male is usually number one in the squirrel community.

But each squirrel knows where it stands in the pecking order. Squirrels save their energy for important tasks—like finding food and avoiding enemies.

Many squirrels do not live very long. Their world is full of enemies. They are always alert for danger.

Watch how a squirrel behaves when a dog comes along. It will probably stay close to a tree. If the dog chases it, the squirrel dashes up the tree trunk. Then it sits on a long branch and scolds the dog.

Wild animals are dangerous enemies of young squirrels. Foxes, weasels, and hawks like to eat them.

Squirrels wander through the park, looking for food on moonlit nights. But they are always watching, always listening. An owl may be perched high in the trees, ready to pounce.

Shade Tail

We have been watching gray squirrels in all seasons. If you had to draw a picture of this wonderful little animal, what would you think of first?

An owl may be perched in a tree, ready to pounce.

You would probably agree with scientists. All over the world, no matter what language they speak, scientists call the gray squirrel by its name in Latin—*Sciurus*. It means "shade tail."

Squirrel watchers spend many hours studying that big, bushy tail. We already know that the tail is as long as all the rest of the squirrel's body. But this tail often tells us a great deal about what the animal is doing and how it feels.

A squirrel's tail is like a big signal flag. When the animal is angry or alarmed, the tail twitches and ripples, like a flag blowing in the wind.

See how fast it goes. Do you think a squirrel's tail twitches faster when it is *very* excited? You're right—it does.

A squirrel has muscles all through its tail. It controls the hairs on its tail with those muscles. They make the hairs stand up straight, or lie flat. Try to figure out what the squirrel is saying with its tail.

We can tell how important the tail is by the amount of time a squirrel spends caring for it. The animal stops often to groom it and keep it fluffy. The squirrel picks out burrs and twigs that are tangled in the hairs.

A squirrel's tail is useful in many ways.

The tail protects a squirrel from all kinds of weather. Watch a squirrel sitting in the rain, holding its tail over its back like an umbrella. When the hairs are soaked, the squirrel shakes the water from them.

In hot sun, a squirrel shades itself with this "beach umbrella." On cold nights, it wraps itself and its babies in this "blanket."

For us, the most fun comes from watching a squirrel depend on its tail in the tall trees. The squirrel uses its long tail as a circus acrobat uses a pole on the high wire—the tail helps to balance the squirrel as it runs along narrow branches.

When a squirrel leaps from tree to tree, the long, powerful tail serves as a rudder. It guides the animal to a safe landing.

When a squirrel drops from a branch to the ground, the big fluffy tail serves as a parachute. It helps to set the animal down softly.

Gray squirrels are almost everywhere. Millions of people have turned squirrel watching into an adventure.

What will your adventure be?

Index